Landes v. Brant

JOHN CATRON

Published in 1851@LANDES V. BRANT

TABLE OF CONTENTS

PUBLISHED IN 1851LANDES V. BRANT

PUBLISHED IN 1851LANDES V. BRANT

IN error to the Circuit Court of the United States for the District of Missouri.

Isaac Landes, a citizen of Kentucky, brought an action of ejectment in the court below, at the October term of 1845, against Joshua B. Brant, a citizen of Missouri, to recover a lot of ground in the city of St. Louis. Plea, general issue.

At the trial of the cause, the plaintiff gave in evidence the following patent:

'The United States of America, to all to whom these presents shall come, greeting:

'Know ye, that there has been deposited in the General Land Office a certificate numbered one thousand one hundred and ninety-three, of the recorder of land titles at St. Louis, Missouri, whereby it appears that, in pursuance of the several acts of Congress for the adjustment of titles and claims to lands, Jacques Clamorgan, under Gabriel Dodier, was confirmed in his claim to a tract of land, containing thirty-four acres and sixty-eight hundredths of an acre, bounded and described in a survey dated October 4th, 1826, as follows, to wit: beginning at a stone, the northeast corner of survey number one thousand four hundred and seventy-three, of forty arpents, for Francis Bissonet; thence north twenty-five degrees and forty-five minutes east, two chains and ninety-two links, to an old stone in a ravine on the east side of Third street, which stone, lying flat in said ravine, was re-inserted by the deputy surveyor, and from which stone the southwest corner of a three-story brick house (in block number sixty-six) bears north eighty-seven degrees east; the northwest corner of a brick house (in block number sixty-five, Barbee's tavern) bears south; the northwest

5

corner of a stone house (in block number twenty-six, Eph. Town's Missouri hotel) bears north sixty-nine degrees thirty minutes east; and a black locust, eight inches in diameter, bears north seventy-three degrees west, distant forty-one links; thence north seventy-five degrees twenty minutes west at eighty-three chains an old stone; at one hundred chains an old stone; one hundred and twenty chains to an old stone, the northwest corner of the present survey, from which a white oak, four inches in diameter, bears north twenty-four degrees west, distant sixteen links; a white oak, three inches in diameter, bears north seventy-five degrees east, distant eleven links; and a red oak, five inches in diameter, bears south forty-two degrees east, distant twenty-two links; thence south twenty-five degrees forty-five minutes west, two chains and ninety-seven links, to a stone, the northwest corner of survey number one thousand four hundred and seventy-three, of Francis Bissonet; thence south seventy-five degrees twenty minutes east, one hundred and twenty chains, to the place of beginning, being in township forty-five north of range seven east of the fifth principal meridian, and being designated as survey number one thousand two hundred and seventy-eight in the state of Missouri. There is, therefore, granted by the United States unto the said Jacques Clamorgan, under Gabriel Dodier, and to his heirs, the tract of land above described. To have and to hold the said tract, with the appurtenances, unto the said Jacques Clamorgan, under Gabriel Dodier, and to his heirs and assigns for every.

'In testimony whereof, I, James K. Polk, President of the United States, have caused these letters to be made patent, and the seal of the General Land Office to be hereunto affixed.

'Given under my hand, at the city of Washington, the 18th day of June, in the year of our Lord 1845, and of the independence of the United States the sixty-ninth.

'By the President,

JAMES K. POLK.

[L. S.]

By J. KNOX WALKER, Secretary.

'Recorded Vol. X., pages 36, 37, 38.

'S. H. LAUGHLIN, Recorder of the General Land Office.'

Also an extract from the minutes of the Commissioners to decide land claims, and c., and a record of a confirmation to Jacques Clamorgan, as follows:

'Wednesday, November 13th, 1811. Board met; present, John B. C. Lucas, Clement B. Penrose, and Frederic Bates, Commissioners. Cer., 1278.

'Jacques Clamorgan, assignee of Esther, mulattress, assignee of Joseph Brazeau, assignee of Gabriel Dodier, claiming one by 40 arpents of land, situate [on] Little Prairie, adjoining the town of St. Louis, produces a concession from St. Ange and Piernas, L. G., dated 23d May, 1772; a transfer from Gabriel Dodier and Joseph Brazeau to Esther, dated 4th November, 1793; from Esther to claimant, dated 2d September, 1794.

'The Board grant to Jacques Clamorgan forty arpents of land, under the provisions of the second section of the act of Congress, entitled 'An Act respecting claims to land,' and passed 3d March, 1807, and order that the same be surveyed conformably to the metes and bounds contained in the report of a survey made for said Dodier, and found in Livre Terrien, No. 2, folio 15. Survey at expense of the United States.

'Board adjourned till to-morrow, nine o'clock, A. M. John B. C. Lucas, Clement B. Penrose, Frederic Bates.

'Recorder's Office, St. Louis, Missouri, December 1st, 1846. I do certify the above to have been truly transcribed from book No. 5, of the Commissioners' minutes, pages 398, 406, and 407, as the same remains of record in this office.

'LOREN SPENCER, U.S. Recorder of Land Titles in the State of Missouri.'

'Louisiana.-Commissioners' Certificate, No. 1278.

'We, the undersigned, Commissioners for adjusting the titles and claims to land in the territory of Louisiana, have decided that Jacques Clamorgan, claiming under Gabriel Dodier, original claimant, is entitled to a patent under the provisions of the second section of the act of Congress, entitled 'An Act respecting claims to land in the territories of Orleans and Louisiana, passed the 3d of March, 1807, for forty arpents, situate in the District of St. Louis, Little Prairie, adjoining the town of St. Louis, by virtue of ten consecutive years' possession, prior to the 20th December, 1803, and order that the same be surveyed conformably to the metes and bounds established in the report of a survey made for said Gabriel Dodier, and found in Livre Terrien, No. 2, folio 15. John B. C. Lucas, Clement B. Penrose, Frederic Bates.

'Recorder's Office, St. Louis, 24th February, 1847. The above is a correct copy of original certificate No. 1278, on file in this office, issued by the board of United States Commissioners therein designated, for ascertaining and adjusting the titles and claims to land in the Territory of Louisiana.

'LOREN SPENCER, U.S. Recorder of Land Titles in the State of Missouri.'

Also a certified extract from the registry of patent certificates, containing the date (February 10th, 1845) and the number (1193) of the certificate issued to Clamorgan, together with a copy of survey made in October, 1826.

The plaintiff also gave in evidence the last will and testament of Jacques Clamorgan, dated 31st October, 1814, and admitted to probate on the 7th of November, 1814, in which, after the payment of his debts and the distribution of 150 piastres to the poor, he devised all his estate to his natural children, St. Eutrope, Apoline, Cyprien Martial, and Maximin, to be divided into five equal parts, of which Maximin was to have two parts and each of the others one part.

Also the last will and testament of Cyprien Martial Clamorgan, dated 27th February, 1827, and admitted to probate on the 27th of May, 1827, in which he devises two lots of ground, situate in block No. 25 in the city of St. Louis, to Henry Clamorgan, second natural son of his natural sister, Apoline Clamorgan, and a lot in the same block to Louis and Louisa, infant children of said Apoline, jointly; also all the interest or estate which he might be entitled to in any lands in the state of Missouri to his sister Apoline and her children, Louis, Henry, and Louisa, and the survivor of them.

Also the last will and testament of Apoline Clamorgan, dated the 11th day of April, 1830, and admitted to probate on the 12th day of May, 1830, wherein she devises to Louis and Louisa, and such other children as might be born to her, all her interest and estate in a lot one hundred and twenty feet front by three hundred feet in depth (conveyed to St. Eutrope, Cyprien Martial, and the testatrix, by Joseph Brazeau for Jacques Clamorgan), being in block No. 25 in the city of St. Louis; likewise any interest or estate she might have in any other lands in the state of Missouri to her children.

The plaintiff also gave in evidence a deed bearing date the 28th day of April, 1845, from Louis and Henry Clamorgan to the plaintiff and one Fidelio C. Sharp, conveying all the interest (except an undivided fourth) which they might have under any patent to be issued by the United States upon the certificate of confirmation dated November 13th, 1811, to Jacques Clamorgan.

It was admitted, on behalf of the defendant, that, at the time of the institution of this suit, he was in possession of a part of the premises described and embraced in the plaintiff's declaration, to wit, a lot in the city of St. Louis, fronting one hundred and eleven feet six inches on Washington Avenue, and running back north one hundred and fifty-two feet in depth, bounded on the south by Washington Avenue and on the west by Fourth Street; and that the said lot is embraced in the confirmation, survey, and patent read in evidence by the plaintiff, being part of that forty arpent tract, which tract is bounded south by the centre of Washington Avenue.

It was proven, on the part of the plaintiff, that it was reported and believed by the near relatives and friends of St. Eutrope and Maximin, that they died many years ago, the former leaving a wife, but no children, the latter having never been married, and both having died intestate.

That Cyprien Martial died in the year 1826 or 1827, and that Apoline died in 1829 or 1830; that Apoline left four children at her death, to wit, Louis, Henry, Louisa, and Cyprien; that Louisa died in 1833 or 1834, being then only seven or eight years old; that Louis, Henry, and Cyprien, her remaining children, are yet living; that Apoline died a few days before the birth of her son Cyprien; that Apoline was never married, and her children were illegitimate; that Cyprien, Martial, and Apoline were mulattoes.

It was admitted on the part of plaintiff and defendant, that Jacques Clamorgan died between the date and probate of his will, as read in evidence by the plaintiff.

The defendant gave in evidence a transcript of a record of the General Court of the Territory of Louisiana, in the case of Gregoire Sarpy, Executor of Antoine Reihl, v. Jacques Clamorgan. In this transcript no return appeared upon the summons. The judgment was rendered 16th May, 1808, and commenced with the usual form, 'And now at this day come the parties aforesaid, by their attorneys,' andc. Execution was taken out and levied on the interest of Clamorgan in a certain lot of land one arpent front by forty arpents in depth (being that now in controversy), and the same was sold at public auction by Jeremiah Connor, the sheriff, to Alexander McNair, and a sheriff's deed given therefor, bearing date the 8th day of July, 1808.

Also a transcript of a record of the Circuit Court of St. Louis County, in the case of Rufus Easton v. Jacques Clamorgan's Executors, setting out a judgment against the defendants, and an execution thereon, and a sale and deed by John K. Walker, sheriff, to John O'Fallon and Jesse G. Lindell, after the following advertisement:

'By virtue of a writ of execution issued from the Clerk's office of the Circuit Court of St. Louis County, and to me directed, in favor of Rufus Easton, against Jacques Clamorgan's executors, I have levied upon, and will sell for cash to the highest bidder, at the court-house door in St. Louis, on Thursday, the 27th day of July instant, between the hours of nine and five, all the right, title, claim, interest, estate, and property, that was of said Clamorgan at the time of his death, in and to a piece or parcel of land, containing one arpent in front by forty arpents in depth, and bounded on the eastern end by a fence formerly made to defend the crops of the inhabitants of St. Louis against the animals or beasts; on the north by land of Tayon (Pere); on the western end by the king's domain or vacant land; and on the south by the highway which leads to the village of St. Charles; it being the same lot of forty arpents acquired by said Clamorgan of Gabriel Dodier, by deed bearing date November 4th, 1793. The boundaries, as above set forth, are the same as given in said deed. Sold to satisfy said execution and costs. St. Louis, July 1st, 1826.

'JOHN K. WALKER, Sheriff.'

To the admission of both these records the plaintiff objected, and, upon the objection being overruled, excepted.

Defendant then read in evidence the following documents, to wit:-1st. A deed from Alexander McNair and wife to Jeremiah Connor. 2d. A copy made by the Spanish Lieutenant-Governor of a deed from Dodier to Esther, with a deed from Esther to William C. Carr indorsed thereon; and 3d. A deed from William C. Carr and wife to Jeremiah Connor, also indorsed on such Spanish copy. 4th. A deed from Jeremiah Connor to George F. Strother. 5th. A deed from George F. Strother to James D. Earl. 6th. A mortgage from James D. Earl to Sullivan Blood. 7th. A deed of release from James D. Earl to Sullivan Blood. 8th. A deed from George F. Strother and wife to Thomas H. Benton, and Thomas Biddle, in trust, andc. 9th. A deed from Thomas H. Benton and Thomas Biddle, and Luke E. Lawless and wife, to Sullivan Blood. 10th. A deed from Sullivan Blood and wife to the defendant.

It was in evidence that Jeremiah Connor had inclosed the Dodier lot soon after the change of government. That Clamorgan went to Mexico in 1806, and returned in 1808 or 1809. There were also in evidence three deeds of emancipation from Jacques Clamorgan to his four children, St. Eutrope, Cyprien Martial, Apoline, and Maximin, all dated 16th September, 1809, in which it was recited that St. Eutrope was born in April, 1799; Apoline on the 7th of February, 1803; Cyprien Martial on the 10th of June, 1803; and Maximin in the beginning of the year 1807.

The following instructions were asked for by the plaintiff:

1. That the legal effect of the patent and confirmation read in evidence by the plaintiff was to vest the legal title to the premises therein mentioned in Jacques Clamorgan, the patentee, if living at the date of the patent, and if not living, then in his heirs, devisees, or assignees, in the same manner as if the patent had issued in the lifetime of said Clamorgan. Given.

2. That prior to the confirmation read in evidence by the plaintiff, the legal title to the premises embraced in said confirmation was in the government of the United States, and that the confirmation, survey, and patent read in evidence by the plaintiff were effectual to vest the legal title to said premises in Jacques Clamorgan, his heirs, devisees, or assignees. Given.

3. That the judgment read in in evidence by the defendant in favor of Gregoire Sarpy, executor of Antoine Reihle, to the use of Mildrum and Parks, against Jacques Clamorgan, was null and void, and the sale made by the sheriff by virtue of the execution issued thereon, and the deed from said sheriff to Alexander McNair, are also null and void. Refused.

4. That the deed from Sheriff Connor to Alexander McNair, dated 8th July, 1808, and read in evidence by the defendant, is void for uncertainty, and should be disregarded by the jury. Refused.

5. That the deed from Sheriff Connor to Alexander McNair, read in evidence by the defendant, is void as to the plaintiff, unless he had notice of said deed at the date of the deed from Louis and Henry Clamorgan to him, as read in evidence by said plaintiff. Refused, and No. 5 (post, p. 357) given.

6. That the sale made by John K. Walker, sheriff, to O'Fallon and Lindell,

on 27th July, 1826, and the deed made in pursuance of said sale, dated 10th August, 1826, as read in evidence by defendant, are fraudulent and void. Rejected.

7. That if, at the date of the levy and sale by Sheriff Walker to O'Fallon and Lindell, the premises levied upon, or a considerable portion thereof, then constituted a part of the city of St. Louis, and had before then been laid off into blocks and squares, separated by streets and alleys, and distinctly marked out by stones set up at the corners, or other visible boundaries, and if some of said lots or blocks had before then been sold and conveyed by Jeremiah Connor, claiming to be the proprietor thereof, and if upon the said lots or blocks, so sold, buildings and other improvements had before then been erected, then the said levy and sale were null and void. Rejected.

8. That if the premises levied upon by Sheriff Walker, by virtue of the execution in favor of Rufus Easton, and sold by said sheriff to O'Fallon and Lindell for thirty-three dollars, were at the time of said levy and sale susceptible of division without injury to the property, and were at the date of said levy and sale worth five thousand dollars or more, then the said sale is fraudulent and void in law. Refused.

9. That the sale made by Sheriff Walker to O'Fallon and Lindell is void, unless the said sheriff in his levy or advertisement, or in the deed to said O'Fallon and Lindell, described the premises sold with reasonable certainty, so that the same could have been indentified by the said description. Given.

10. That if the premises in controversy are embraced by the confirmation and patent read in evidence by the plaintiff, the sale and conveyance from Sheriff Connor to Alexander McNair, read in evidence by defendant, were not operative to convey the legal title to said McNair, and the said sale and conveyance cannot prevail as against the patent and confirmation in this action.

This instruction as asked for is refused, for the reason that it involves confusion; we are of opinion that the legal title to the premises embraced by the sheriff's deed was in the United States until the patent issued, provided the deed covers the land in dispute; but that the imperfect title owned by Clamorgan did pass by the sheriff's deed made by Connor to McNair, 8th July, 1808; and that neither the act of confirmation by the Board of Commissioners in 1811, nor the issuance of the patent in 1845, defeated the title made by Sheriff Connor in 1808; and so the jury are instructed.

11. That the deed from Gabriel Dodier to Esther, and the deed from Esther to William C. Carr, and the deed from William C. Carr to Jeremiah Connor, read in evidence by defendant, did not at the date of the said last-mentioned deed vest in the said Connor any title to the premises in dispute which can prevail in this action; provided the same premises had before then been confirmed to Jacques Clamorgan, and have since been patented to him by the government of the United States. Given.

12. That the possession by the defendant, or those under whom he claims, of the premises in controversy, in order under any circumstances to constitute a valid bar to the plaintiff's recovery, must have been an actual, adverse, and uninterrupted possession for the space of twenty years next preceding the institution of this suit.

This instruction is given, although not strictly as asked.

13. That if, at the dates of the sale and conveyance from Sheriff Connor to Alexander McNair, read in evidence by defendant, the premises conveyed in said deed were susceptible of a description by which the same might have been identified with reasonable certainty, and if the same were not so described either in the levy or sheriff's deed, then the said deed is void, and vested no title in McNair.

This instruction involves one matter of law, appertaining to the decision of the court on a motion heretofore made to reject the sheriff's deed, and overruled; and therefore the instruction is refused; but the jury are instructed that it is their duty to find whether the land described in the sheriff's deed is the land in dispute in this action, and the same land that was confirmed to Jacques Clamorgan; and if the land in dispute is not the same land conveyed by the sheriff's deed and confirmed as aforesaid, then said deed cannot furnish a defence to this defendant.

14. That if, at the date of the levy and sale by Sheriff Connor to Alexander McNair, read in evidence by defendant, Jacques Clamorgan owned two tracts of land, each of them containing one arpent in front by forty in depth, both situated in the Little Prairie and adjoining the then town of St. Louis, then the deed from Sheriff Connor to Alexander McNair, read in evidence by defendant, is void for uncertainty.

This instruction is refused, because there was no legal evidence given to the jury, either proving, or tending to prove, that on the 8th of July, 1808, Jacques Clamorgan was the owner of two such tracts of land.

15. That the execution in favor of Rufus Easton against the executors of Jacques Clamorgan, dated the 3d day of April, 1826, and read in evidence by the defendant, and all the proceedings of the sheriff under and by virtue of that execution, are null and void. Refused.

16. If the jury find from the evidence that the boundaries described in the deed from John K. Walker, sheriff, to John O'Fallon and Jesse G. Lindell, given in evidence by the defendant, were not, at the time of the sale by the said sheriff, the true boundaries of the tract of one by forty arpents that had been confirmed to Jacques Clamorgan, as mentioned in the certificate and record of confirmation given in evidence by the plaintiff, and that the same has not been bounded in the manner stated in said deed for a period of more than twenty years, and that the deed referred to in the said description contained in said sheriff's deed, as the one from which it was taken, had no existence in fact, then the said description is insufficient, and said sheriff's

deed from Walker is void; unless the jury shall find from the evidence, that the said tract of one by forty arpents was generally known in the community at the date of said sale by the description given in said deed.

This instruction is refused, and the jury instructed instead thereof, that they must find the land in dispute was covered by Sheriff Walker's deed to O'Fallon and Lindell, before that deed can avail the defendant as an outstanding title.

17. That the deed, given in evidence by the defendant, from Jeremiah Connor, sheriff, to Alexander McNair, conveyed no title to said McNair to the tract of one by forty arpents mentioned in the confirmation, of the Board of Commissioners of date November 13th, 1811, given in evidence by the plaintiff. Refused.

And thereupon the court gave the 1st, 2d, 9th, 11th, and 12th instructions, and refused to give the remainder, but in place of the 5th gave the following:

5. The unregistered deed made by Sheriff Connor to McNair on the 8th of July, 1808, was valid, as between Clamorgan, the execution debtor, and McNair, the purchaser; and equally so as against the devisees of Clamorgan, without being recorded. But it was not valid as against a purchaser of the same premises from Clamorgan's devisees, who purchased for a valuable consideration, and without notice of the existence of the deed of 1808.

The deed on which the plaintiff relies was made in April, 1845, and if the plaintiff then had actual notice of the deed of 1808, it was valid also as to him, without having been recorded. And if the jury find that the defendant Brant was in the open and notorious possession and occupation of the premises when the deed of 1845 was made, and had been so for years before that time, continuously holding under the deed of 1808, then this is evidence from which, connected with other circumstances, the jury may find that the plaintiff had actual notice of the existence of the deed of 1808, when he took his deed in 1845. And so the jury are instructed.

And in place of the 10th, gave the following: 10. This instruction, as asked for, is refused, for the reason that it involves confusion; we are of opinion that the legal title to the premises embraced by the sheriff's deed was in the United States until the patent issued, provided the deed covers the land in dispute; but that the imperfect title owned by Clamorgan did pass by the sheriff's deed made by Connor to McNair, 8th July, 1808; and that neither the act of confirmation by the Board of Commissioners in 1811, nor the issuance of the patent in 1845, defeated the title made by Sheriff Connor in 1808, and so the jury are instructed.

And in place of the 13th, gave the following:

13. This instruction involves one matter of law appertaining to the decision of the court, on a motion heretofore made to reject the sheriff's deed, and overruled, and therefore the instruction is refused; but the jury are

instructed that it is their duty to find whether the land described in the sheriff's deed is the land in dispute in this action, and the same land that was confirmed to Jacques Clamorgan; and if the land in dispute is not the same land conveyed by the sheriff's deed, and confirmed as aforesaid, then said deed cannot furnish a defence to this defendant.

And in place of the 16th, gave the following:

16. This instruction is refused, and the jury instructed instead thereof, that they must find the land in dispute was covered by Sheriff Walker's deed to O'Fallon and Lindell, and before that deed can avail the defendant as an outstanding title.

To the refusal of which several instructions as asked for, the plaintiff at the time excepted.

The defendant then moved the court for the following instructions:

1. If the jury find from the evidence that the tract of land sold and conveyed by Jeremiah Connor, sheriff, to Alexander McNair, in 1808, as the property of Jacques Clamorgan, is the same tract of land which was claimed by said Clamorgan before the Board of Commissioners, and confirmed to him, then the confirmation to said Clamorgan enures to said Alexander McNair and those claiming under him. Given.

2. If the jury find from the evidence that the lot in dispute is embraced in the tract of land sold and conveyed by John K. Walker, sheriff, to Jesse G. Lindell and John O'Fallon, in 1836, by virtue of the judgment and execution in favor of Rufus Easton against the executors of Jacques Clamorgan, then the plaintiff is not entitled to recover. Given.

3. If the jury find from the evidence that the defendant, and those under whom he claims, have been in possession of the lot in controversy for twenty years consecutively, prior to the commencement of this suit, and since Apoline Clamorgan and Cyprien Martial Clamorgan, under whom the plaintiff claims, arrived at the age of twenty-one years, that such possession was under a claim of title adverse to the plaintiff and those under whom he claims, then the issue ought to be found for the defendant. Given.

To the giving of which the plaintiff objected, but the court overruled the objection, and gave each of said instructions, to which the plaintiff excepted at the time.

Verdict for plaintiff, and judgment thereon, upon which this writ of error was sued out.

The cause was argued by Mr. Bradley, for the plaintiff in error, and by Mr. Gamble, for the defendant in error.

Mr. Bradley, for the plaintiff in error.

First Point. The legal title being clearly in the plaintiff, the first question arises under the tenth instruction, in which it is submitted there is error.

1st. An exception was reserved to the admissibility of this deed in evidence; because the record of the cause is either imperfect, or, if perfect, it shows the judgment is void.

It is not an erroneous judgment. There could be no jurisdiction without an appearance. The recital in the judgment, 'And now at this day come the parties aforesaid, by their attorney,' andc., is simply surplusage. That could not give life to a void act. There was no service of process, no plea filed, no appearance in person or by attorney, no issue, no evidence. Smith v. Ross, 7 Miss., 463; Hollingswoth v. Barbour and others, 4 Pet., 466, 472; Anderson v. Miller, 4 Blackf. (Ind.), 417; Shaefer v. Gates, 2 B. Mon. (Ky.), 453; Englehead v. Sutton, 7 How. (Miss.), 99.

If the judgment is void, it may be objected to in a collateral proceeding. Campbell v. Brown, 6 How. (Miss.), 230.

It was not a judgment by confession, nor want of a plea.

Again, there is evidence to show that Jacques Clamorgan was not at St. Louis at the time the writ issued, or between that time and the time at which the judgment purports to have been entered. He left there in 1806, and returned in the winter of 1808, or spring of 1809. The writ issued 6th April, 1808; Judgment, 16th May, 1808; execution, 6th June, sale, 8th July, 1808.

2d. If the judgment was valid, yet the deed was inoperative and void as to subsequent bona fide creditors and purchasers, without actual notice, if it was not recorded within the time prescribed by law. This is admitted in the instruction. Where there is no record, there must be actual notice. 1 Territorial Laws (Edward's Comp.), p. 47, § 8; Frothingham v. Stocker, 11 Mo., 3.

3d. But the court below say further, if the jury find the defendant Brant was in open and notorious possession and occupation of the premises, andc., 'then this is evidence from which, connected with other circumstances, the jury may find the plaintiff had actual notice.'

It is submitted that there is error in this last clause of the instruction. Undoubtedly there might be other circumstances which, taken in connection with the possession, would justify such finding, but it was an abstract proposition eminently fitted to mislead the jury.

Second Point. In the plaintiff's fifth and defendant's first instructions, there is error.

1st. The proposition there is, that the imperfect title held by Clamorgan before the confirmation was transferred by the sheriff's deed to McNair, and the subsequent confirmation and patent to Clamorgan enured to the benefit of McNair.

1. If the imperfect title passed by that deed, the purchaser could and ought to have perfected it before the Commissioners. 12 Pet., 454, 458.

2. It was property. Soulard et al. v. U. States, 4 Pet., 511.

3. The decision of the Commissioners, confirming the claim, is conclusive as to all parties having antecedent rights. U. States v. Percheman, 7 Pet., 86;

Strother v. Lucas, 12 Id., 458; Chouteau v. Eckhart, 2 How., 357; U. States v. King, 3 Id., 787; Hickey v. Stewart, Id., 759, 760; Newman v. Lawless, 6 Mo., 290; Mackay v. Dillon, 7 Id., 13.

4. The deed is as to Clamorgan in invitum. It is without covenant of any kind, and but a conveyance, against his will, of such title as he then had. He was not bound to perfect it.

5. A deed operates by relation, or enures to the benefit of another, only where he who receives the deed has led the other into an interest in the property, and to avoid injury to that interest from events happening between the creation of that interest and the execution of the deed, or the first and second delivery of the deed. 4 Kent Com., 454, 555; 4 Johns. (N. Y.), 230; 15 Id., 316; 1 Cow. (N. Y.), 613.

6. If McNair had, under the sheriff's deed, and imperfect title, and was bound to have perfected it, and Clamorgan was under no obligation to have it confirmed, and afterwards procured a confirmation to himself in his individual right, it vested in him the legal title and equitable interest, paramount to any intermediate equities created against his will.

But 2d. The court refused to instruct the jury that the deed from the sheriff was void for uncertainty in the description of the property. It is a sale under execution. Hart v. Rrctor, 7 Mo., 534, and cases there cited; Evans v. Ashley, 8 Id., 177; 1 J. J. Marsh. (Ky.), 33. See the cases cited.

Third Point. The plaintiff's ninth and defendant's second instructions relate to the second record, judgment, execution, and sheriff's sale. The plaintiff submits there is error in these instructions, as also in the refusal to give the instructions refused. An exception was reserved to this deed.

1st. It was a suit and judgment against an executor, 'and that he have his execution against the goods and chattels, lands and tenements, which were of said Jacques Clamorgan,' andc.

The execution follows the judgment.

Although the judgment may be simply erroneous, and therefore not now to be called in question, it cannot justify the execution. The Revised Code of Missouri, 1825, p. 112, §§ 49, 50, provides for the classification of debts, and p. 563, for the classification or marshalling of the assets.

The personal estate should have been first subjected. Gantley's Lessee v. Ewing, 3 How. 707; 1 Blackf. (Ind.), 210.

2d. If the execution was properly issued, the deed did not describe the property with reasonable certainty. No deed from Gabriel Dodier to Clamorgan is shown to help out the defective description, nor was there in fact any such deed. See cases above. Besides, the land had then been laid off, divided into blocks and squares, and lots, and streets and alleys, and the description was wholly delusive.

3d. The property sold for $33 to satisfy $27.88, leaving a surplus of $512. The property was worth $10,000, if free from encumbrance. It was capable of division, and was, in fact, divided. It was evidently taken in connection with the previous sale under another execution, intended to get up all the interests of all Clamorgan's heirs in all his property within the jurisdiction of the court. Taking all the circumstances together, it was strong evidence of fraud, and ought to have been left to the jury on that ground. Tiernan v. Wilson, 6 Johns. (N. Y.) Ch., 417; 4 Cranch, 403; 18 Johns. (N. Y.), 362; 6 Wend. (N. Y.), 522; 3 Blackf. (Ind.), 376.

Fourth Point. The instruction granted by the court, as to adverse possession, left to the jury a mixed question of law and fact. The plaintiff submits that it is erroneous.

1st. Because it submitted to the jury to find whether the possession was adverse, without qualification.

The defendant claimed under the two sheriff's deeds. If those deeds were void, no length of time would create an adverse possession.

A sheriff's deed which is void for want of jurisdiction in the court under whose judgment the sale took place, is not such a conveyance as that a possession under it will be protected by the statute of limitations. Walker v. Turner, 9 Wheat 541-551; Powell's Lessee v. Harman, 2 Pet., 241; Hoskins v. Helm, 4 Litt. (Ky.), 310; Brooks v. Marbury, 11 Wheat., 90; 9 Johns. (N. Y.), 167; 1 Id., 157.

2d. The deed from Sheriff Walker to O'Fallon and Lindell is within twenty years of the bringing of the suit. By claiming under that deed, the defendant is estopped to deny that the title was then in the heirs of Clamorgan. 14 Johns. (N. Y.), 225, and note.

The court had previously ruled these deeds to be good. If they were void, no adverse possession could arise. Yet the whole question of adverse possession was left to the jury.

Adverse possession is a legal idea, admits of a legal definition, of legal distinctions, and is therefore correctly laid down to be a question of law. Bradstead v. Huntington, 5 Pet., 402, 438.

The judge did not define the legal properties necessary to constitute an adverse possession, and the facts stated in his instruction do not of themselves constitute such adverse possession.

3d. The statute of limitations of Missouri cannot avail the defendant.

1. The deed of 10th August, 1826, admits the title of plaintiff's ancestor, and there is no proof of actual adverse possession for twenty years before, and continuously down to suit brought.

2. Louis and Henry Clamorgan, under whom the plaintiff claims, are within the saving of the statute of 1818. Territorial Laws, 598.

Finally. The plaintiff maintains, that, although there may have been an equitable title in the defendant, and under the statutes of Missouri an action of ejectment may be maintained on an equitable title in that state, yet such title cannot prevail against the legal title. It is conceded that the legal title is in the plaintiff, and it is insisted by defendant that it is held in trust for him. This is an implied trust. If it exists at all, it arises from some wrongful act of the plaintiff, or those under whom he claims. But it is begging the question to say the act was wrongful, and must enure to the benefit of defendant. It was the object of the commission to settle the rights of conflicting claimants. It was entirely within the power of McNair or O'Connor to have brought this question before them. The transactions were then fresh, and no difficulty would have occurred in adjusting any controversy between them. On these grounds, effect is given to the confirmation to pass the legal title. A conclusive effect is necessarily given to such confirmation, unless it be in cases of fraud and wrong.

If there be an equity in those claiming under the said judgments, it cannot prevail in a court of law as against the legal title; and the substance of the instructions given by the court is, it is respectfully submitted, wrong in that particular. Chouteau v. Eckhart, 2 How., 375; Hickey v. Stewart, 3 Id., 750; United States v. King, 3 Id., 787; Les Bois v. Bramell, 4 Id., 449.

Mr. Gamble, contra.

Clamorgan had filed his claim with the Recorder of Land Titles, and the same was pending before the Board of Commissioners, prior to the year 1808. The fifth section of the act of Congress of the 3d of March, 1807 (2 Stat. at L., 440), had limited the time for the exhibition of claims to the 1st of July, 1808. There was no mode provided by law for substituting for the claimant an heir, devisee, or assignee, who had acquired the right of the claimant after his claim was filed. Clamorgan claimed to be the legal representative of Gabriel Dodier, by purchase from Esther, who purchased from Brazeau, who purchased from Dodier, the original grantee. In July, 1808, the sheriff, under execution, sold the interest of Clamorgan in the land, and executed his deed to McNair, the purchaser. The thing itself, so filed, in which Clamorgan claimed an interest, whilst it was sub judice, was sold; and his interest, as it then existed, was sold, namely, a Spanish claim which had been filed. The sheriff's deed is declared by the law under which it was made to be effectual 'to pass to the purchaser all the estate and interest which the debtor had, or might lawfully part with, in the land, at the time the judgment was obtained.' Edwards's Territorial Laws, p. 121, § 45. The purchaser at sheriff's sale held a conveyance which was as operative to pass Clamorgan's interest in the land, as any instrument which Clamorgan himself could have made. He was by that deed constituted the sole representative of Gabriel Dodier, the original grantee of the land.

As to the objection of want of an appearance, the Supreme Court of Missouri have decided that hardly any state of circumstances would justify them to set aside a sheriff's sale, where possession had followed the deed. Tindell v. Bank, 4 Mo., 228; Landis v. Perkins, 12 Id., 254; Day v. Kerr, 7 Id., 426. It is then the settled law of Missouri, that, under the recital contained in this judgment, the defendant will be held to have appeared. No matter whether Clamorgan was in Mexico or not.

If we look to the practice under the Spanish authorities, and since, we shall find that these claims were not a contingent interest separate from the estate, (as was the case in Blanchard v. Brooks, 12 Pick. (Mass.), 52,) but were a present existing interest in the land, and were susceptible of transfer and every form of conveyance. And in whatever form the claimant's interest was conveyed, his claim to the confirmation was conveyed.

It is said that the purchaser should have filed his sheriff's deed with the Board, and claimed the confirmation to himself. But this could not be done. The law limited the time within which claims could be filed. That time had passed before this sale was made.

The patent which conveyed the legal title, being issued in the name of Clamorgan, who was then dead, passed the legal title to the person who was then the holder of the equitable title previously in Clamorgan, and the purchaser of that equitable title would take the legal title, under the patent, in preference to a devisee of Clamorgan. 5 Stat. at L., 31; Act of 3d March, 1807 (2 Stat. at L., 440).

The language of the Commissioners has probably induced musapprehension. They 'grant,' andc., although they had no power to grant. The acts of Congress makes the grant, and the Commissioners were only to ascertain, by rules of evidence, whether the claim was a valid one, according to the laws of Congress.

The language, then, which may be employed by the Board, does not, in any manner, affect the operation of the confirmation. If the words in this case had been, 'the claim filed by Jacques Clamorgan is confirmed,' or, 'the Board are of opinion that the claim filed by Jacques Clamorgan is a valid claim,' the effect would have been precisely the same as is produced by the language actually employed, 'the Board grant to Jacques Clamorgan,' andc.

The doctrine of relation applies here with all its force. The Commissioners act upon the claim as filed. They act upon it as it was when filed. The Commissioners in this case having to decide upon claims throughout what is now Missouri, Iowa, and Wisconsin, the adjudication would necessarily be long delayed, and would present just such a case as would make the doctrine of relation applicable.

A judgment relates to the first day of the term at which it is rendered. A deed executed in pursuance of an agreement to convey may relate back to the time of the contract. Jackson v. Bard, 4 Johns. (N. Y.), 230. A sheriff's deed relates back to the day of sale. Jackson v. Dickinson, 15 Johns. (N. Y.), 309; Boyd v. Longworth, 11 Ohio, 235. An acknowledgment of a deed relates back to the time of its execution. 8 Ohio, 87. So the confirmation relates back to the filing of the claim.

As to the objection that the lands ought not to have been sold before the goods and chattels. How can that be inquired into collaterally in the case of a sheriff's sale? What has the purchaser to do with the question whether the sheriff has made proper search for goods and chattels before he sells the land? There is no evidence here that there was any personalty at all. The objection is raised merely from the form of the precept.

It was objected to the instruction as to possession, that the court ruled, that from open and notorious possession, 'connected with other circumstances,' the jury might infer that the plaintiff had notice, andc. In Missouri, circumstances are considered sufficient to prove actual notice. Before a jury it would be competent to contend that circumstances made out a case of notice. Possession is one circumstance. A list made out in Clamorgan's handwriting (this lot being omitted) is another. And so on. The gist of the instruction was, that the jury might find from circumstances that the plaintiff had actual notice; not that the circumstances detailed were proof of notice.

A question was made in the court below in relation to the sufficiency of the description contained in the sheriff's deed to McNair. The plaintiff contended that the deed was void for uncertainty, and objected to its being admitted in evidence, and afterwards moved for instructions to the jury to the same effect. In the fourth instruction, the court was asked to declare, as a matter of law, that the deed was void. This instruction the court very properly refused, as it required the court to pass upon all the facts in evidence before the jury, relating to the description contained in the deed. The thirteenth instruction, which applies to the same subject, was refused by the court in the form in which it was asked, but in lieu of it the court instructed the jury, 'that it was their duty to find whether the land described in the sheriff's deed is the land in dispute in this action, and the same land that was confirmed to Clamorgan, and if the land in dispute is not the same land conveyed by the sheriff's deed, and confirmed as aforesaid, then said deed cannot furnish a defence to this defendant.'

This instruction refers the question to the jury, whether the description in the sheriff's deed covers the land in dispute. They are to take the deed with its description, and all the evidence describing the land in dispute, and to determine whether the description in the deed embraces the land in controversy. The Supreme Court of Missouri, in the case of Landis v. Perkins, 12 Mo., 260, say:-'Whether the description of the premises sold was sufficient, would depend upon extrinsic circumstances. If the lot was known by the description given, the sale would be valid, according to the principles settled in the case of Hart v. Rector, 7 Mo., and parol evidence was admissible to establish that fact.'

The Circuit Court, undoubtedly, gave the proper instruction, to direct the attention of the jury to the question of fact upon which the validity of the deed depended, and very properly refused to instruct the jury that this deed was void for uncertainty.

If it were necessary to cite authorities to show that descriptions, as general as that used in this deed, have been held to be sufficient, I would refer the court to 4 Dev. and B. (N. C.), 414; 1 Humph. (Tenn.), 80; 3 Yerg. (Tenn.), 171; 7 Id., 490; 8 Gill and J. (Md.), 349; 2 N. H., 284.

Mr. Bradley, in reply and conclusion.

There is a wide difference, as to adverse possession, between a claim of title from the same stock under a defective deed, and a claim of title from another stock. In the former case, if the deed under which the claim is set up is void, it nevertheless admits the title of the other. That is the case here. If we show that the deeds of the sheriff are void, they purporting to convey Clamorgan's title, do we not thereby confirm as against them the title under which they claim? Is it not an admission that our title is good, unless it has been divested by the machinery on which they rely? The cases cited show that possession under a void deed is a possession consistent with, and subordinate to, the title of the true owner, and can never give rise to an adverse title.

Now as to what passed by the sheriff's deeds, I maintain that nothing passed but the naked possessory title:-'All the estate and interest which the debtor had, or might lawfully part with, in the land, at the time the judgment was obtained.' See Edwards's Ter. Laws, p. 121, § 45. Now what had Clamorgan at that time which he 'might lawfully part with' in this land? I do not ask to what he might by proper covenats bind himself. But what had he which could have passed by a mere quitclaim deed?

He had then an equitable interest in the land, which is said to have been the subject of seizure and sale. He had, also, a claim pending before the Board of Commissioners, for a confirmation of that interest, so as to create in him a legal estate. Was that, also, the subject of seizure and sale? Would that pass by a quitclaim deed? The claim was before the Board. It is said the time for filing claims had passed. Was there anything to prevent the assignee, if he were such, from filing his assignment made subsequent to the filing of that claim? Clearly he might have done so. Clamorgan was there. His was a mere possessory title, with an inchoate right to the legal estate. His possessory right was the subject of seizure and sale. It was a valuable thing, and, unless some one else procured the legal estate, it might be perfected. The means of perfecting it were within his reach. The law of this court is, that however strong the possessory right, however clear the equity, a grant or confirmation to a stranger claiming the land would have passed the legal estate to such stranger. There was, then, every motive to induce him to present his claim to a confirmation, if he had one, and it might then have been decided, when every thing was fresh, and the parties on the spot. The law provided for legal representatives, and embraced as well those who were assignees before, as after, the claim filed. It was confirmed to Clamorgan.

It is supposed the legal title enured to the benefit of the intermediate assignee of Clamorgan, that is, to the forced assignee, after the claim filed. Upon what principle? Was Clamorgan bound by any legal or moral obligation to perfect the title? The sheriff had sold his possession; no more. Illustrations are drawn from the law of relation, which is supposed to be clearly expouded in the books, and cases are put forth to show its operation; a deed executed in performance of an agreement, a judgment, a sheriff's deed, the acknowledgment of a deed, are put; to which may be added the case of Graham v. Graham, 1 Ves., 275, and Garnons v. Knight, 8 Dowl. and Ry., 348. In these and like cases, where a man, by his own voluntary act, has passed an imperfect title to another for a full consideration, and afterwards seeks to transfer the property to another, or that interest is sought to be subjected by process to his debts, or he has, after a full consideration received, or under covenant, received a good title, in such case, the law, to prevent injustice, interposes, and by relation secures the title to the first vendee. But there is a wide distinction between voluntary and compulsory acts, between a naked quitclaim and a covenant for title, between a mere right to present possession and enjoyment and an absolute estate in fee. In the case of a naked quitclaim, an after-acquired title will never relate back, so as to vest in the vendee of the quitclaim. 1 Cow., 613. Nor would any court tolerate for a moment, that a squatter who has the bare possession, and sells that, should be debarred from acquiring for himself the absolute estate in fee. And there is a substantial reason for this distinction. He who buys an imperfect title pays a proportionate price for it. He has no right to look to his vendor to complete it. He takes it for what it is worth; no more. I admit that the same rule of relation applies to sheriff's deeds, and to others acting in a fiduciary or executive capacity, where the title to the property has passed by the sale, and the deed is a mere formal execution of the power. In some states, Maryland for instance, the deed from the sheriff is not necessary, nor is it in cases of chancery sales; and when executed, it relates back to the time of the sale. But what does it convey? Has it ever been supposed to carry with it any thing more than the actual title or interest which the party had at the time of such sale? If this rule prevails as between vendor and vendee, where they deal together, and treat of the actual right or possession, the thing in esse not in posse, it should apply with still greater force to a case where the sale is wholly in invitum. The policy of the law and the rules of courts are much more stringent in such cases than in those where the parties act voluntarily.

Here the whole proceeding against Clamorgan was compulsory. He had an interest which could be taken in execution. The confirmation was most uncertain, at best. The claim was not appraised. It was not in any manner referred to. The purchaser was bound to know that he was buying but a naked possession, and he must, of course, have regulated his price by that. There was, then, no foundation even for equity to interpose to compel a deed from Clamorgan. And will it be pretended, that courts of law will make a deed enure by relation, when equity would not interpose to compel the party to make it?

The great questions in this case are as to the effect of the confirmation and patent; whether or not the confirmation and patent enure to the purchasers at the sheriff's sale, or, the deeds of the sheriff being void, whether the title does not subsist in the heirs and devisees of Clamorgan.

The cases cited from the fourth and sixth volumes of the Missouri Reports differ from this. In the first there was process served and an appearance by attorney. In the last there was service of process on one of the defendants. Here there was no service of process, no appearance.

But it is thought the defects are cured by the entry, that 'the parties come by their attorneys,' andc., and the record is not to be contradicted; it binds parties and privies, is a solemn judgment of a court of competent jurisdiction, final and conclusive until reversed. If it is a record, it must stand or fall by itself. It does not require the aid of the maxim cited for its support. But is it a record, and as such entitled to conclusive force? The judgment begins with 'Therefore it is considered,' andc. The rest is recital. No court can have jurisdiction except under certain statutes, unless the defendant is before it. On the return of process, an attorney may appear if the defendant is in court, but I know no case in which an attorney has been allowed to appear suo motu, unless the party was in court. There must be an authority, clear and explicit, naming the attorney, or there must be a party in court under process. Here there is neither. It is a mockery of justice, not error, but absolutely void, to allow a voluntary appearance by attorney without any authority of record, or the presence of the party in court. There is nothing in the whole proceedings from which it can be inferred that the defendant had notice, actual or constructive, of this proceeding, and without this the judgment is a nullity. See the cases on the brief, and also Buckmaster v. Carlin, 3 Scam. (Ill.), 104, and Crane v. French, 1 Wend. (N. Y.), 312. A case in 6 Miss., 50, and one in 7 Id., 426, are relied on to show that such a recital binds the parties. But these cases, if they are in conflict with, are clearly overruled by, 7 Miss., 465. If the rule is so inflexible, it would never be in the power of the defendant to show that he had no notice.

Nor does the maxim, 'Ex diurnitate temporis omnia presumuntur, rite et solemniter esse acta,' apply to such a case. That can avail only where there is a defect in the proof, and to supply the imperfect record. But when the proof is itself a matter of record, and no suggestion is made of a defect in it, not evanescent, but fixed and public, courts must deal with it alone, and not with presumptions.

Nor is the ruling of the court sustained by the passage in Greenleaf, nor the case in Wendell, on which the defendant relies. It is not a case of an erroneous judgment; but of a judgment utterly void for want of jurisdiction over the person of the defendant, for want of an appearance under process, or by any voluntary authority. It is not sought to reverse or vacate it, but to treat it as a nullity; and this may be done in a collateral proceeding as well as in any other mode.

Mr. Justice CATRON delivered the opinion of the court.

The first title paper offered in evidence by the plaintiff was a patent from the United States to Jacques Clamorgan, dated June 18, 1845, which purports to grant 'to said Clamorgan (under Gabriel Dodier), and to his heirs,' the land in dispute.

The patent is founded on a certificate made by the first board of commissioners established at St. Louis, which declares, that Clamorgan, claiming under Dodier, original claimant, was entitled to a patent under the provisions of the second section of the act of Congress of 3d March, 1807; and it was ordered that the same should be surveyed conformably to the metes and bounds established in the report of a survey made for said Gabriel Dodier, 'and found in Livre Terrien, No. 2, folio 15; by virtue of ten consecutive years' possession, prior to the 20th December, 1803.' The confirmation and certificate bear date November 13th, 1811.

According to the former decisions of this court, all controversy was concluded by the confirmation as regarded two questions:-First, it settled that Clamorgan was the true and proper assignee under Dodier, through the various mesne conveyances by which Clamorgan claimed. Bissell v. Penrose, 8 How., 330. Secondly, that Clamorgan had the oldest and best claim to the land, as against every other claimant under the Spanish government. In explanation of our former decisions, it is proper to remark, it is held, that, as between two claimants under that government, setting up independent imperfect claims, the courts of justice had no jurisdiction; that in such cases it appertained to the political power to decide to whom the perfect title should issue; and when this was done, no controversy could be raised before the courts of justice impeaching this first confirmation. [6]

The only question decided in Chouteau v. Eckhart, 2 How., 345, and in Les Bois v. Bramell, 4 Id., 449, was, that when Congress confirmed and completed an imperfect claim, and then confirmed another and different claim for the same land, the older confirmation defeated the younger one; nor could a court of justice go behind the first confirmation, and ascertain from facts and title papers which claimant had the better original equity. That if this was allowed, then the first confirmation could be overthrown by the courts; and the action of the political department (in all cases of double confirmation) would have no conclusive force when the courts were resorted to.

In the present case, the plaintiff's right of recovery cannot be questioned on the face of his title; and the controversy depends on the defendant's claim of title. In 1808, Sarpy recovered a judgment against Clamorgan in the District Court at St. Louis, for $2,393. The objection to the judgment is, that no process seems to have been served on Clamorgan, and it is proved that he was absent in Mexico at the time; but the record of the judgment states, that 'now at this day came the parties by their attorneys, and neither of said parties requiring a jury, but this case with all things relating to the same being submitted to the court, for that it appears to the court that said Sarpy has sustained damages,' andc. And then a judgment follows.

A defendant's being beyond the jurisdiction of a court is not conclusive evidence that the judgment was void; he may have left behind counsel to defend suits brought against him in his absence, by which means his property could be reached by attaching it; and the proof shows it to be probable enough that such was Clamorgan's condition when the judgment was rendered. But the validity of the judgment does not depend on this consideration. If it was voidable for want of notice, and a false statement on its face, 'that the parties appeared by their attorneys and dispensed with a jury, and submitted the facts to the court,' then it should have been set aside by an audita querela, or on petition and motion; such being the familiar practice in similar cases. [7]

Furthermore: This suit in ejectment is collateral to the judgment; and it cannot be impeached collaterally. So the Supreme Court of Missouri held in 1848, in the case of Landes v. Perkins (12 Mo., 254), on the same title, and a similar record in all respects to that before us, and with the views on this point there expressed we entirely concur.

In the same case it is held that Clamorgan's interest in the land by virtue of his imperfect Spanish claim was subject to seizure and sale under execution, according to the then laws of Missouri; that the proceeding was not void, but passed to the purchaser at execution sale all the title that would have passed from Clamorgan, had he made a quitclaim deed to McNair, the purchaser.

That such was the force and effect of a regular sheriff's deed under the local laws of the then Missouri territory is not open to question; nor is it controverted. And the only remaining consideration on this branch of the case is, whether the sheriff's deed can be set up as a defence at law, notwithstanding the confirmation and patent, both of which are of subsequent date to the sheriff's sale and deed.

The court below held, that the title set up in defence under the sheriff's sale was a valid, legal title; and so charged the jury; which instruction was excepted to; and this presents the principal matter of controversy now before us.

Clamorgan's claim to the land sold had existed for many years before the

United States acquired Louisiana. It had been regularly surveyed, by order of the Spanish government, and the survey was filed with the recorder, according to the act of 1805; Clamorgan had held possession under the claim of Dodier, to the extent of his survey, for more than ten consecutive years, before the 20th of December, 1803; he was on that day in possession, and then a resident of Louisiana.

The second section of the act of March 3, 1807, declares, that any person thus claiming and holding land shall be confirmed in his title to the tract thus held. The confirmation was to be made by the commissioners; and by section fourth their decision was to be final against the United States in cases within the foregoing description. And section sixth provides that a patent shall issue on a certificate of the Board.

In the case of Landes v. Perkins, the Supreme Court of Missouri held that the conclusive legal title vested in Clamorgan by the confirmation of 1811; and that, being the date of the legal title, a court of law could not go behind it; nor did the confirmation, or patent, relate to any previous step taken to acquire title; and the sheriff's deed, being a mere quitclaim, did not estop Clamorgan or his devisees from setting up the legal title against such a deed. And it is intimated that a court of equity could be resorted to, and through its aid the sheriff's sale might be set up by decree.

How far a court of equity would interfere in such a case we are not disposed to inquire, as it is apprehended that the Supreme Court of Missouri was mistaken in the effect it attributed to the confirmation of 1811, and the patent founded on it. Clamorgan's petition asking a confirmation (under the act of 1805) was filed with his title papers with the recorder; and they were recorded (December 10, 1805).

The imperfect title as then filed was subject to seizure and sale by execution; the ultimate perfect title demanded and granted was a confirmation and sanction by the political power of the imperfect title, and gave it complete legal validity; and to protect purchasers, the rule applies, 'that where there are divers acts concurrent to make a conveyance estate, or other thing, the original act shall be preferred; and to this the other acts shall have relation,'-as stated in Viner's Abr., tit. Relation, 290. The doctrine of relation is well illustrated in Jackson v. M'Michael, by the Supreme Court of New York, 3 Cow., 75, and recognized by the Supreme Court of Missouri in the case of Crowley v. Wallace, 12 Mo., 145.

Cruise on Real Property (Vol. V., pp. 510, 511) lays down the doctrine with great distinctness. He says: 'There is no rule better founded in law, reason, and convenience than this, that all the several parts and ceremonies necessary to complete a conveyance shall be taken together as one act, and operate from the substantial part by relation.' [8]

For the purposes of this case, (without proposing to apply the rule to every other,) we may assume that the first act of Clamorgan was that of filing his title papers and claim with the recorder of land titles, according to the fourth section of the act of March 2, 1805; this was regularly done, and the papers recorded. He claimed under the second section of the act of 1805, which was amended by the act of April 21, 1806, and again by the act of March 3, 1807. As already stated, by the fourth section of this last act, the decision of the board of commissioners appointed to investigate such claims is made final against the United States, and he was entitled to a patent. His claim was fully within the provisions of the acts of 1805 and 1807.

Applying the doctrine of relation, and taking all the several parts and ceremonies necessary to complete the title together, 'as one act,' then the confirmation of 1811, and the patent of 1845 must be taken to relate to the first act; that of filing the claim in 1805. On this assumption, intermediate conveyances made by the confirmee, or by the sheriff on his behalf, of a date after the first substantial act, are covered by the legal title, and pass that title to the alienee. And on this ground the deed made by the sheriff to McNair is valid.

But there is another consideration equally conclusive in favor of the sheriff's deed in the present instance. Clamorgan died in 1814; and by his will devised his lands to his illegitimate children, under whom the plaintiff Landes claims title. In 1845, a patent issued purporting to convey to Clamorgan, in fee simple, the land in dispute; according to common law rules, the patent was void for want of a grantee; and to supply this defect, Congress passed a general law (May 20, 1836), declaring, 'That, in all cases where patents for public lands have been, or may hereafter be, issued, in pursuance of any law of the United States, to a person who had died, or who shall hereafter die, before the date of such patent, the title to the land designated therein shall enure to, and become vested in, the heirs, devisees, or assignees of such deceased patentee, as if the patent had issued to the deceased person during life.'

Of course the assignee by a bona fide conveyance would come in before a volunteer, such as an heir or devisee. Here the assignee of the devisee is suing the alienee of the devisor. The patent issued in 1845 is the ultimate and conclusive evidence of title in this instance, as the board of commissioners had no power to grant and communicate the fee held by the United States. Their decision was final, to this extent; the officers of government were bound to award the patent to Clamorgan, without any further action on the part of Congress. But this adjudication does not stand on the footing of cases where the commissioners were ordered to report, and Congress reserved the power to confirm the report, and thus to grant the fee by act of Congress; in such cases, this court has held that Congress had granted the fee, and that no patent was required as a further assurance of title. To what description of assignee, then, did the title enure according to the act of 1836? Necessarily to one claiming, not the legal, but the equitable title, existing when the patent issued; and in him the legal title is vested by the patent. The same rule was applied in the case of Stoddard v. Chambers, 2 How., 316. In 1800 a concession was made to Mordecai Bell; in 1804, Bell conveyed to James Mackay; and in 1805, Mackay conveyed to Amos Stoddard, whose heirs were the plaintiffs. The claim was filed with the board in 1808, and in 1836 it was confirmed to Mordecai Bell 'and his legal representatives.' This court held, on the foregoing state of facts, 'that when, under the act of 1836, the report of the commissioners was confirmed to Bell and his legal representatives, the legal title vested in him, and enured by way of way of estoppel to his grantee, and those who claim by deed under him. [9] There was no covenant for title in either the assignment from Bell to Mackay, or in that from Mackay to Stoddard, each being quitclaim assignments.

So, again, in the case of Bissell v. Penrose, 8 How., 317, the same principle was maintained. In August, 1800, Tillier filed his claim with the board, and asked a confirmation for 800 arpents; and it continued before the different boards sitting at St. Louis until 1836, when it was confirmed by Congress. In 1818, Tillier assigned his claim to Clement B. Penrose; and in 1820, Penrose assigned his claim, acquired from Tillier, to Mary B. and Anna Penrose, who were the plaintiffs in the ejectment suit, and who recovered the land, under their deed of 1820.

In every case when this court has been called on to investigate titles, where conveyances of lands had been made during the time that a claim was pending before a board of commissioners, and where the claim was ultimately confirmed in the name of the original claimant, the intermediate assignments have been upheld against the confirmee, and his heirs or devisees, in the same manner as if he had been vested with the legal title at the date of conveyance. We are therefore of opinion, that the sheriff's deed made to McNair in 1808 must be supported on this ground also.

The second objection to the sheriff's deed is, that it was not recorded when Landes purchased from Clamorgan's devisees. The Circuit Court instructed the jury, that, as between the devisees and those claiming under McNair, the deed was valid without recording, but that it was not valid to defeat a subsequent bona fide purchaser without notice of its existence; and further instructed the jury, that, 'the deed on which the plaintiff relies was made in April, 1845, and if the plaintiff then had actual notice of the deed of 1808, it was valid also as to him, without having been recorded. And if the jury find that the defendant Brant was in the open and notorious possession and occupation of the premises when the deed of 1845 was made, and had been so for years before that time, continuously holding under the deed of 1808, then this is evidence from which, connected with other circumstances, the jury may find that the plaintiff had actual notice of the existence of the deed of 1808, when he took his deed in 1845.'

The material objection to the charge is, that other circumstances taken in conection with the adverse holding were required to exist, in the opinion of the court, and that these circumstances are not enumerated. And our opinion is, that if more had been required than the open and notorious adverse possession and occupation of the premises, and the court had given an instruction in general terms as above set forth, it would be erroneous. [10] If, however, the possession alone was sufficient, then the general terms 'connected with other circumstances' were prejudicial to the defendant, and fall within the general rule 'that a man cannot reverse a judgment for error, unless he can show that the error was to his disadvantage.' 3 Bac. Abr., Error, K., 105.

And this brings us to the question, whether open and notorious occupation and adverse holding by the first purchaser, when the second deed is taken, is in itself sufficient to warrant a jury or court in finding that a purchaser had evidence before him of a character to put him on inquiry as to what title the possession was held under; and that he, the subsequent purchaser, was bound by that title, aside from all other evidence than such possession and holding. It is conclusively settled in England, that open and notorious adverse possession is evidence of notice; not of the adverse holding only, but of the title under which the possession is held. Hiern v. Mill, 13 Ves., 120; Daniels v. Davison, 16 Id., 253; per Eldon, Lord Chancellor.

And in the United States we deem it to be equally settled. The cases in New York will be found in Gouverneur v. Lynch, 2 Paige (N. Y.), 300, and in Grimstone v. Carter, 3 Id., 436, per Walworth, Chancellor. In Kentucky, in Brown v. Anderson, 4 Litt. (Ky.) 201, and Buck v. Holloway, 2 J. J. Marsh. (Ky.), 180. Nor are we aware that a contrary doctrine is held in any state in the Union. We are therefore of opinion, that the charge given on this point was correct, so far as the plaintiff in error is allowed to call it in question.

The next inquiry arises on the refusal of the Circuit Court to charge the jury that the sheriff's sale made by John K. Walker (sheriff), in 1836, was void. The executors of Clamorgan were sued, and a recovery had against them, as executors, by Rufus Easton; and the premises in dispute were sold, and under this sale the defendant also claims title. That the lands of the deceased debtor could be seized and sold under the judgment according to the then laws of the state of Missouri, we hold to be free from doubt; so the Supreme Court of that state held in the case of Landes v. Perkins, (12 Mo.) above referred to, and in which case all the points in controversy on this branch of the title were discussed, and in our judgment properly decided; the opinion there given is in conformity to the instructions given and refused in the court below, in this case, and in which we hold there was no error.

There is no other question presented by the record requiring examination, and it is therefore ordered that the judgment of the Circuit Court be affirmed.

This cause came on to be heard on the transcript of the record from the Circuit Court of the United States for the District of Missouri, and was argued by counsel. On consideration whereof, it is now here ordered and adjudged by this court, that this cause be, and the same is hereby, affirmed, with costs.

www.ingramcontent.com/pod-product-compliance
Lightning Source LLC
Chambersburg PA
CBHW070756180526
45168CB00004B/1640